Handle
WITH
Care

AN UNUSUAL
BUTTERFLY
JOURNEY

LOREE GRIFFIN BURNS

photographs by
ELLEN HARASIMOWICZ

M MILLBROOK PRESS/MINNEAPOLIS

FOR CASSIDY AND CAEDAN,
who love butterflies
—*L.G.B.*

FOR PAUL, who lifts my
wings and helps me soar
—*E.H.*

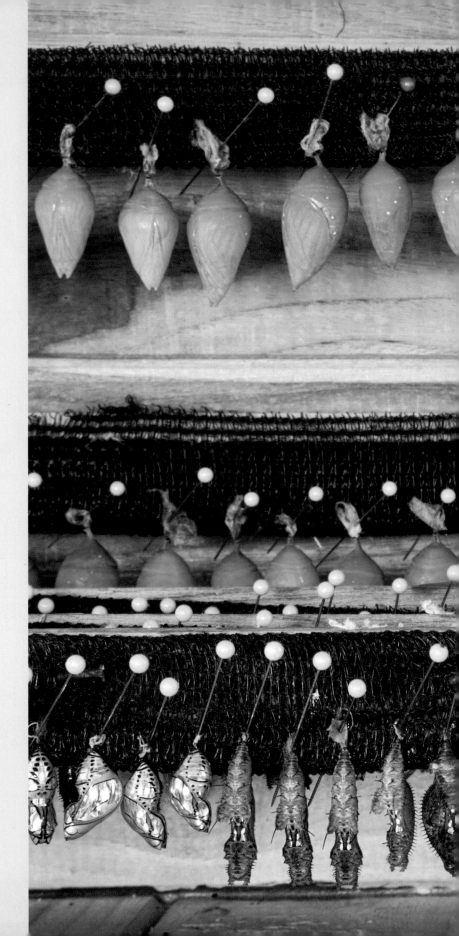

The author would like to thank Dr. May Berenbaum and Dr. Tom Turpin for sharing their expertise on all things entomological.

Text copyright © 2014 by Loree Griffin Burns
Photographs copyright © 2014 by Ellen Harasimowicz

Diagrams on pages 5 and 7 © Laura Westlund/Independent Picture Service.

Additional images are used with the permission of: © E.R. Degginger/Science Source, p. 28 (middle left and middle right); © Dwight Kuhn, p. 28 (bottom left); Cyndi Souza/U.S. Fish and Wildlife Service, p. 28 (bottom right).

Main body text set in Adrianna Regular 13/20. Typeface provided by Chank.

Millbrook Press
A division of Lerner Publishing Group, Inc.
241 First Avenue North
Minneapolis, MN 55401 U.S.A.

For updated reading levels and more information, look up this title at www.lernerbooks.com.

Library of Congress Cataloging-in-Publication Data
Burns, Loree Griffin.
   Handle with care : an unusual butterfly journey/ Loree Griffin Burns ; Photographs by Ellen Harasimowicz.
      pages cm
   Includes index.
   ISBN 978–0–7613–9342–9 (lib. bdg. : alk. paper)
   ISBN 978–1–4677–2542–2 (eBook)
   1. Butterflies—Juvenile literature. 2. Butterfly farming—Costa Rica—Juvenile literature. I. Harasimowicz, Ellen, photographer. II. Title.
QL544.2.B79 2014
595.78'9—dc23   2013018086

Manufactured in the United States of America
1 – DP – 12/31/13

A **M**YSTERIOUS PACKAGE has arrived at the museum. It's shiny and has traveled a long, long way. It's sturdy. And it's *inside* this silver box . . .

De/ From: **Mariposario del Bosque**
Santa Cecilia de la Cruz de Guanacaste,
Costa Rica, CENTRAL AMERICA

Inside the silver package, a museum worker finds a rectangular block of foam filled with butterfly pupae.

IT'S A PUPA!
WHAT'S A PUPA?

Well, it's one part of a four-part insect life. The first part is an egg. A larva hatches from the egg. The larva transforms into a pupa. Finally, the pupa becomes an adult. Insects that live these four-part lives include beetles, flies, bees, moths, and butterflies.

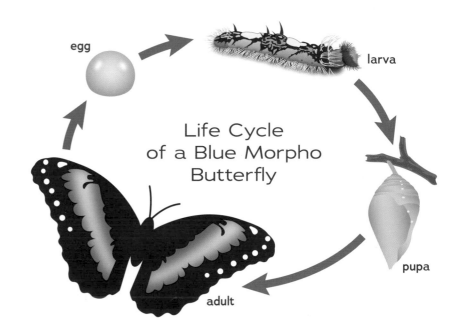

Life Cycle of a Blue Morpho Butterfly

egg

larva

pupa

adult

This is a butterfly pupa. Some people call it a chrysalis. Really, though, it's an ingenious package. Inside its sturdy skin, a butterfly larva—you might call it a caterpillar—is quietly changing into an adult.

But hold on. Why is this happening in a museum?

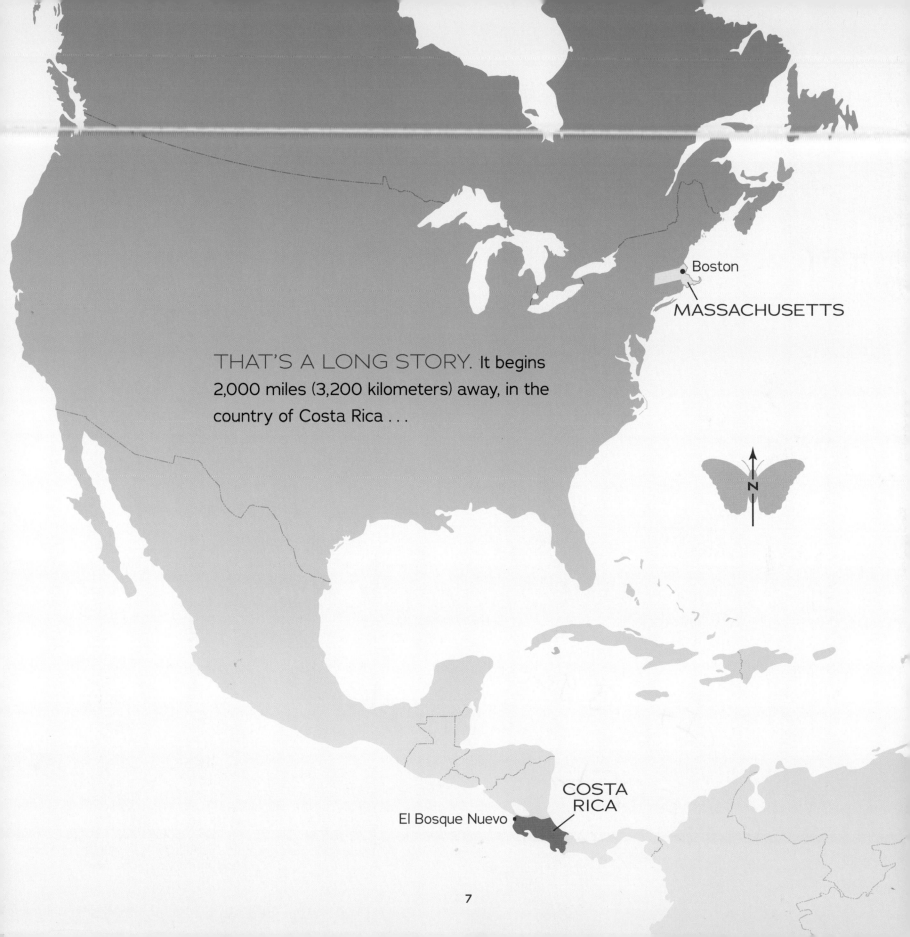

THAT'S A LONG STORY. It begins 2,000 miles (3,200 kilometers) away, in the country of Costa Rica . . .

Boston

MASSACHUSETTS

N

COSTA RICA

El Bosque Nuevo

LIKE ALL BUTTERFLY LIFE STORIES,
this one begins with a mother butterfly laying an egg.

Since blue morpho caterpillars can only eat leaves from certain pea plants, blue morpho mothers will only lay eggs on those plants. Each egg will hatch a single tiny blue morpho caterpillar.

Unlike most mother butterflies, this one lives in a greenhouse.
She was moved here from the nearby forest so that she could lay
her eggs inside the greenhouse's tall, screened walls.

The greenhouse is on a farm called El Bosque Nuevo. The farmers here don't grow carrots or potatoes or cucumbers. They grow butterfly pupae. They sell the pupae to museums so that people around the world—people like you and me—can learn more about butterflies. The farmers use the money they earn to protect the forest around their farm.

The dirt road leading to El Bosque Nuevo cuts through a tropical forest. You can see three greenhouses and the roof of the main house on the left side of the road, near the middle of the photograph.

TO A CATERPILLAR, LIFE IN A GREENHOUSE IS NOT MUCH DIFFERENT FROM LIFE IN A FOREST. The larva spends its days eating leaves . . . and growing. When it gets too big for its own skin, the too-small outer layer—called an exoskeleton—splits. Underneath is a new, larger exoskeleton. This process is called molting.

Raising thousands of growing caterpillars keeps the farmers at El Bosque Nuevo busy. Their most difficult job is making sure the caterpillars always have fresh leaves to eat. A crop of several hundred caterpillars can eat an entire greenhouse of leaves in just a day or two. The farmers must be ready to bring in new plants when they are needed.

Left: A herd of hungry caterpillars has eaten this plant down to branches and leaf stems. The farm hand is moving the stranded caterpillars (not visible) by hand.

Facing page: If you look closely at the leaves in this image, you'll spot a herd of young blue morpho caterpillars. There are so many that if you stood next to this tree with your eyes closed, you would hear the caterpillars chewing!

The farmers have other chores too. They provide plates of crushed bananas and cups of sugar water for the adult butterflies in the greenhouses.

A farmer puts colored sponges in the cups of sugar water to give the butterflies places to perch.

The farmers also work hard to keep animals from sneaking in. Some animals want to eat the caterpillars and butterflies. (Birds! Frogs! Snakes!) Others want to eat the greenhouse plants. (Grasshoppers!) So the farmers make sure there are no holes in their screens. And they make sure the grounds around the greenhouses are free of leaves, branches, and other debris that could hide small animals.

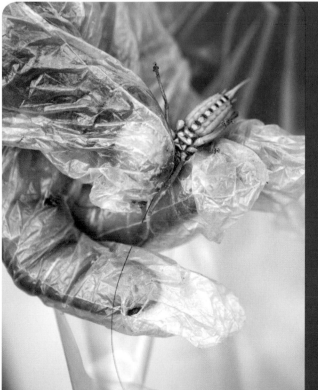

Above: Farmhands search the greenhouses every day, leaf by leaf, for caterpillar-eating critters.

Left: Grasshoppers sneak into the greenhouses despite screened walls and watchful farmers.

Right: Pupae farmers sometimes use the tools of a more traditional farmer, like shovels and spades.

The caterpillars pay no attention to all this fuss. They just eat and grow and molt, eat and grow and molt. For most species, molting simply produces larger and larger caterpillars.

For others, like the blue morpho, molting results in caterpillars with new color patterns and hairlines. These changes tell the farmers which caterpillars are ready to become pupae.

Each day, farmers search for older caterpillars in the greenhouses. They pick the ones they find and move them to a place where they can be watched more closely.

THIS PLACE, CALLED THE PUPARIUM, is lined with screened cabinets. Each cabinet is crawling with caterpillars. The farmers provide fresh leaves for those caterpillars that still need food.

For those that have stopped eating, the farmers supply the only thing they do need: a safe place to hang.

Each caterpillar chooses a spot and marks it with silk produced inside its own body. The final task of the caterpillar stage of life is to attach itself firmly to this silk.

Ready-to-pupate caterpillars explore the interior of a cabinet. The puparium houses a variety of butterfly pupae, including the four species shown to the right.

At every hour of every day, dozens of caterpillars pupate. No longer caterpillars, not yet butterflies, the pupae are now something in-between.

STURDY AND TIGHTLY SEALED, THESE INGENIOUS PACKAGES ARE READY TO TRAVEL.

Some pupae don't go far. They stay at El Bosque Nuevo. A few of the butterflies that emerge from these pupae are released back into the forest. The farmers return others to the greenhouse, where they will mate. Their eggs will become the farm's next generation of caterpillars.

A farmhand releases farm-raised butterflies back into the greenhouse.

But most of the pupae take a longer journey. These are
sorted and wrapped gently in cotton and tissue paper.

They are packed in cardboard, covered in protective foil, and delivered to the airport. Although the pupae don't need food or water to survive their trip, they are alive. They must be handled with care. And they must arrive at their final destination before this stage of life ends.

Packages like the one being sealed above are bundled together and delivered to the airport *(below)*, where they will eventually be loaded onto planes.

Five days after leaving the farm in Costa Rica, a blue morpho pupa hangs from a pin in the Museum of Science in Boston. For two more weeks, it remains there, quiet and mysterious. THEN, SUDDENLY, IT CHANGES . . .

INSECTS AND THEIR LIFE CYCLES

Would you believe that there are more than nine hundred thousand different kinds, or species, of insects on this Earth? One way to organize this huge number of insects into groups is by looking at the way their bodies change during their lifetimes.

Butterflies, as you've just read, undergo **complete metamorphosis**. The caterpillar that hatches out of a butterfly egg looks nothing like an adult butterfly. Through the process of molting and, most especially, pupating, it eventually takes on a completely changed adult form.

Other insects, like grasshoppers, undergo **simple metamorphosis**. A grasshopper egg hatches a tiny insect that looks just like an adult grasshopper, only smaller. This tiny grasshopper is called a nymph. It change slightly as it grows and molts, eventually becoming a full-sized adult grasshopper.

Still other insects, including dragonflies, undergo **partial metamorphosis**. Dragonfly larvae, called naiads, look nothing like adult dragonflies. They spend their lives in the water. The change to adult form happens suddenly and without a pupal stage. One day, the dragonfly is a full-grown naiad with no wings. The next, it has molted into an adult dragonfly.

These transformations are amazing to watch. Keep your eyes on insects, and you just might witness them for yourself.

INSECT WORDS

In this book, you've learned that the simple four-stage life of a butterfly can be described in this way:

egg ► **larva** ► **pupa** ► **adult**

But since a butterfly larva can also be called a caterpillar and a butterfly pupa can also be called a chrysalis, the four-stage butterfly life cycle can be written this way too:

egg ► **caterpillar** ► **chrysalis** ► **butterfly**

There are other insects with four-part lives, though, and many of them have special names for the life stages, too. A fly larva, for example, is called a maggot. That means the four-part life cycle of the fly can be written like this:

egg ► **larva** ► **pupa** ► **adult** or

egg ► **maggot** ► **pupa** ► **fly**

A beetle larva is known as a grub. So the four-part life cycle of the beetle can be written like this:

egg ► **larva** ► **pupa** ► **adult** or

egg ► **grub** ► **pupa** ► **beetle**

These are just a few of the words used to describe insect life cycles. There are many more. And that's not all. There are unusual words to describe insect body parts (have you ever seen a proboscis?), insect habits (do you know what eclosion is?), and even the people who make insects their hobby (they're called entomologists). Learning or reading about these words can feel overwhelming at first. But don't worry! All the insect words you've read in this book can be found in the glossary on the next page. And the many, many insect words you haven't read here will be fun to learn later, as you continue to explore the incredible world of insects.

GLOSSARY

chrysalis: another word for the butterfly pupa, the third stage of the four-part butterfly life cycle.

eclosion: the emergence of an adult insect from its pupal case; the images on the bottom of page 26 show the eclosion of a blue morpho butterfly.

entomologist: a person who studies insects

exoskeleton: the rigid outer shell of an insect body. The exoskeleton of a growing insect is shed in a process called molting.

larva: the second stage of a four-stage insect life cycle. This life stage is sometimes given a specific name for certain insects. For example, a butterfly larva is also called a caterpillar and a fly larva is also called a maggot. The plural is larvae (LAHR-vee).

larval: describes something as being related to a larva, as in a *larval* life stage

metamorphosis: a change, as in the changes of an insect's body plan during the course of its life

molting: in insects, the process of replacing an outgrown exoskeleton with a newer and larger one

naiad: the aquatic (living in the water) larval stage of certain insects

nymph: the terrestrial (living on the land) larval stage of certain insects

proboscis: the elongated mouthpart of certain insects; you can see a butterfly proboscis on page 8.

pupa: the third stage of a four-stage insect life cycle. This life stage is sometimes given a specific name for certain insects. For example, a butterfly pupa is also called a chrysalis. The plural is pupae (PYOO-pee).

pupal: describes something as being related to a pupa, as in a *pupal* life stage

puparium: at El Bosque Nuevo, the name given to the screened house designed especially for housing older caterpillars and pupae

pupate: the process of becoming a pupa

LERNER
SOURCE

Expand learning beyond the printed book. Download free, complementary educational resources for this book from our website, www.lerneresource.com.

FURTHER READING

BOOKS

Bishop, Nic. *Butterflies and Moths*. New York: Scholastic, 2009.

Burris, Judd, and Wayne Richards. *The Life Cycles of Butterflies: From Egg to Maturity, a Visual Guide to 23 Common Garden Butterflies*. North Adams, MA: Storey, 2006.

Heos, Bridget, and Stephane Jorisch. *What to Expect When You're Expecting Larvae: A Guide for Insect Parents (and Curious Kids)*. Minneapolis: Millbrook Press, 2011.

Kelly, Irene. *It's a Butterfly's Life*. New York: Holiday House, 2007.

WEBSITES

North American Butterfly Association (NABA)
http://www.naba.org/
Many state and regional NABA chapters have their own websites, which will be an excellent source of information about the butterflies you can expect to see in your own backyard.

Bugguide
http://bugguide.net
This is a wonderful site to visit when you've found a butterfly or other insect that you can't identify.

VISITING A LIVE INSECT EXHIBIT

The International Association of Butterfly Exhibitors and Suppliers keeps an online list of its members, which include insect houses and butterfly pavilions around the world (see http://iabes.org/memberfacilities.htm). A web search for phrases like "butterfly house" or "insect zoo" plus the name of your state is another easy way to find exhibits. For example, if you search for the words *butterfly house Massachusetts*, you'll find the Museum of Science in Boston, where some of the pictures in this book were taken.

If you do visit a live butterfly exhibit, be prepared . . . Bring binoculars, a camera, or paper and pencil to help see and record your trip. You will almost certainly come across butterflies that were raised on farms like the one described in this book. Most exhibits will even have pupae on display. If you're lucky, you'll be able to watch a new butterfly emerge from its chrysalis.

Live butterfly enclosures are warm and humid, since those are the conditions tropical butterflies prefer. Although the butterflies themselves are quiet, don't be surprised to hear blowers pumping heat and sprinklers misting the air.

You will not be allowed to touch butterflies, but looking at them closely is encouraged. As you walk through the exhibit, watch for butterflies at your feet, at eye level, and even near the ceiling.

Continued on the next page.

You'll surely see cups of sugar water and plates of fruit like the ones used in El Bosque Nuevo. Butterflies visiting these feeding stations are great subjects for drawings or photos. (But don't let your shadow pass over the butterfly. You might scare it into flight.)

If a butterfly happens to land on you, don't worry. It won't hurt you. Just take a deep breath and enjoy the experience. If you are ready to leave and the butterfly is still hanging on, ask someone who works at the exhibit to help you remove it. Most exhibits include mirrors at the exits. Before you leave, make sure there are no hitchhikers on your backside!

SELECTED BIBLIOGRAPHY

Much of the information in this book was gathered while living with, watching, and learning from the farmers at El Bosque Nuevo in Guanacaste, Costa Rica. Additional details were drawn from reading books on butterflies and insects, most especially these favorites:

Eaton, Eric R., and Kenn Kaufman, *Kaufman Field Guide to Insects of North America*, New York: Houghton Mifflin, 2007.

Pyle, Robert Michael, *National Audubon Society Field Guide to North American Butterflies*, New York: Knopf, 1981.

INDEX

AUTHOR'S NOTE

In February 2010, Ellen and I were given an amazing opportunity. Lea Morgan, assistant curator of the Butterfly Garden at the Museum of Science in Boston, was traveling to Costa Rica to visit a farm that provided butterflies for her exhibit. She invited us to tag along. And so we had the great fortune of living and working at El Bosque Nuevo. Twice. These were adventures neither of us will ever forget. We woke each morning to the screams of howler monkeys, shared shower facilities with a bat, saw more snakes than we care to remember, hiked through a rainy forest in search of wild butterflies, and spent long hours watching hard working and meticulous farmhands raise their caterpillar crops. We are grateful to Lea and to Ernesto Rodriguez, farm manager, for their hospitality and many kindnesses, and to each of the families we met at the farm. Thank you for sharing your stories with us, and thank you for sharing your pupae with the world.

Some of the farmers at El Bosque Nuevo include *(back row)* Jesus, Victor, Ernesto, Heiner, Andrey, Wilbert, *(front row)*, Karen, Michael, Mercedes, and Floh, the dog.